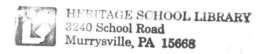

Julie Krone

Bill Gutman
AR B.L.: 5.3
Points: 1.0

Overcoming the Odds

Julie Krone

Bill Gutman

RSVP

RAINTREE
STECK-VAUGHN
P U B L I S H E R S
The Steck-Vaughn Company

Austin, Texas

Published by Raintree Steck-Vaughn Publishers,
an imprint of Steck-Vaughn Company

Developed for Steck-Vaughn Company by
Visual Education Corporation, Princeton, New Jersey
Project Director: Paula McGuire
Editor: Marilyn Miller
Photo Research: Marty Levick
Electronic Preparation: Cynthia C. Feldner
Production Supervisor: Barbara A. Kopel
Electronic Production: Maxson Crandall, Lisa Evans-Skopas, Christine Osborne
Interior Design: Maxson Crandall

Raintree Steck-Vaughn Publishers staff
Editor: Helene Resky
Project Manager: Joyce Spicer

Library of Congress Cataloging-in-Publication Data
Gutman, Bill.
    Julie Krone / Bill Gutman.
      p.   cm. — (Overcoming the odds)
    Includes bibliographical references and index.
    Summary: Traces the life of Julie Krone and discusses her achievements in the
world of horse racing.
    ISBN 0-8172-4121-3
    1. Krone, Julie—Juvenile literature.   2. Jockeys—United States—Biography—
Juvenile literature.   3. Women jockeys—United States—Biography—Juvenile
literature.   [1. Krone, Julie.   2. Jockeys.   3. Women—Biography.]   I. Title.
II. Series.
SF336.K76G87   1996
798.4´0092—dc20
[B]   95–26080
                                                                                              CIP
                                                                                               AC

Printed and bound in the United States
1 2 3 4 5 6 7 8 9 0   99 98 97 96 95

Table of contents

Chapter 1

Top of the World

The 13 horses were nervous as they moved into the starting gate. The jockeys were also nervous. The Belmont Stakes was one of the biggest races of the year. It was the third leg, or race, of the Triple Crown. The other two races were the Kentucky Derby and the Preakness Stakes.

The Triple Crown races are the most important for three-year-old horses. They are also important for the jockeys. Only the best jockeys are chosen to ride in a Triple Crown race.

Julie Krone looked at the 1993 Belmont Stakes as the most important race of her life. It was the 125th year the Belmont was held. No woman jockey had ever finished first.

Julie was riding a very large bay horse by the name of Colonial Affair. At 4 feet 10.5 inches and 100 pounds, Krone was a strange sight on top of the 1,200-pound horse. She almost looked out of place. But those who knew Julie Krone also knew she was

Julie and Colonial Affair in the winner's circle after winning the 125th running of the Belmont Stakes.

one of the toughest and most courageous riders in the country.

On this June 5, 1993, Julie Krone was exactly where she wanted to be. After she mounted Colonial Affair, Julie leaned forward and said to him, "Let's go out and make some history."

The Belmont is one and one-half miles. That's a long distance for a horse race. But Colonial Affair was a good distance horse. Julie knew she didn't have to go to the front right away. Early in the race she hung back. But she was not too far back.

That day the track was muddy. Like all top jockeys, Julie had to think about how her horse would run in the mud. At the top of the backstretch, the side opposite the homestretch, she took Colonial Affair wide to the outside. Later, she explained why.

"You don't want horses to get so much dirt in their face that they become discouraged," she said.

As the race continued, Julie felt the power of Colonial Affair under her. Heading into the far turn, the turn leading into the last, or home, stretch, she knew her horse was in great shape. By the half-mile pole, Julie could feel Colonial Affair pushing forward on his own. She knew she had a great chance to win.

"I said, 'Now he's ready,'" Julie explained later. "No horse was running as strong as my horse."

On the final turn, the last turn of the race, Julie let Colonial Affair loose. There were four horses in front of him. Colonial Affair swept past them. The huge crowd screamed and cheered as Julie drove Colonial Affair home. She opened up a big lead over the second-place horse. The finish line loomed ahead. Julie thought back to a day in 1978 when she had watched the Belmont on television.

"I thought, 'I am going to win the race I watched on TV when I was a kid,'" she said. "It was like a dream come true."

Julie pats Colonial Affair after they cross the finish line to win the Belmont Stakes on June 5, 1993.

Julie and Colonial Affair crossed the finish line. They were two-and-a-half lengths in front. The victory was much more than a dream come true. Julie became the first female jockey ever to win the Belmont. She was also the first woman ever to win a Triple Crown race.

After the race, a tired Julie stood in the winner's circle. She was covered with mud. There were tears of joy in her eyes as the crowd continued to applaud. Julie was on top of the world.

But it wasn't always that way. Julie Krone had to overcome many obstacles to reach the top of her profession. First, she had to overcome being a woman in a man's sport. Then it was a matter of just conquering the sport and avoiding injuries. Sometimes it seemed as if she was always fighting the odds— and winning.

But it wasn't over yet. Julie didn't know it then, but she would soon be facing the most difficult test of her life.

Chapter 2

Born to Ride

Julie Krone's talents were evident from the very beginning. She is one of those people who actually learned to ride a horse before she learned to walk.

Julieann Louise Krone was born July 24, 1963, in Benton Harbor, Wisconsin. She was the second child of Judi and Donald Krone. Their first child was her brother Donnie. Julie's family lived on their own horse farm in nearby Eau Claire, Michigan. So Julie was around horses from the day she was born.

Mrs. Krone raised and rode show horses. She was very good at it. Mr. Krone was a photographer and teacher. Family life at the Krones centered around animals, especially horses. Before Julie could even walk, her mother had her up in the saddle with her.

That was just the beginning. Little Julie was always busy looking for something to ride. First it was Twiggy, the family dog. Then it was the goat, and next the pig.

Her mother could see that Julie was born to ride very early. "When she was two I had her on a pony and was leading him around the farm with a lead rope, no bridle," Judi Krone remembered. "I dropped the rope for a moment, and the pony really took off, bucking like crazy. But Julie's little butt never left his back—and she was laughing."

Julie's mother entered her in horse shows when she was five years old. Julie began winning early on. She competed in shows for nearly 10 years. At 14, Julie was riding in about 33 shows a summer. She won in almost every category they had.

In 1978, something happened to make Mrs. Krone realize that her daughter wasn't going to follow in her footsteps as a show rider. The hottest jockey in the United States was 18-year-old Steve Cauthen. Cauthen had won both the Kentucky Derby and the Preakness Stakes on a horse named Affirmed.

The Belmont was the next big race. If Cauthen and Affirmed could win, they would have won the Triple Crown. That was something few horses and riders ever achieve.

On that warm summer afternoon, Julie sat with her parents watching the Belmont. It was one of the most exciting races ever. Affirmed and a horse named Alydar raced alongside each other for nearly the entire one-and-one-half-mile distance. There was never more than a neck separating them.

Steve Cauthen rode a great race. He never let Alydar ease ahead of Affirmed. Cauthen brought his horse home the winner by a slight margin. By winning the Belmont, they had won the Triple Crown.

Julie decided to be a jockey after seeing Steve Cauthen win the Triple Crown on Affirmed in June 1978. Here Affirmed is on the outside in the third race of the Triple Crown, the Belmont Stakes. Cauthen is wearing number 3.

Young Julie Krone was one of many who marveled at that race. When it ended, she turned toward her mother.

"Mom," she said, "I'm going to be a jockey."

Both Judi and Don Krone knew that being a jockey was not easy for anyone. It was especially difficult for a woman. Yet they also saw that young Julie had a very strong will. If she wanted to be a jockey, she would be one.

Soon Julie marked off a track at their farm. All winter, she rose at 6 A.M. and rode before school. She often rode in the snow.

Because she was small even then, Julie had an advantage. Jockeys should not be too big or weigh too much.

Soon just racing horses around the farm wasn't enough. Julie had to taste the real thing. In 1979, Julie was a junior at Eau Claire High School. During spring break, Julie had her mother drive them to the famous Churchill Downs racetrack in Louisville, Kentucky. That's where the Kentucky Derby is run. Julie started looking for a job at the track.

Veteran trainer Clarence Picou gave her a job during spring break as a "hot walker." That meant Julie walked the horses that had just come off the track after a race. Horses must be walked until their temperatures and heart rates return to normal.

Julie loved being around the track. After school let out that summer, she returned to Churchill Downs. Her mother even changed the date on Julie's birth certificate so that Julie appeared to be the working age of 16. Picou then hired her for the summer. He also found her a place to stay.

Julie was finally where she had always wanted to be. She knew she had a long way to go to become a jockey. She was also aware that it would be even tougher for a woman. The odds were against her. But she had already written her ambition in her diary.

Julie wrote, "I'm going to be the greatest jockey in the world."

Chapter 3

A Woman in a Man's World

Julie Krone had chosen to enter a profession that was basically closed to women for more than 100 years. She began to actively pursue her career in 1979. It had been only ten years since the first woman mounted a horse to race against the men.

In the late 1960s, a show rider named Kathy Kusner applied for a license to become a jockey. She was denied because she was a woman. Kusner had to sue to gain her license. She got it, but somehow never raced.

Then, on February 7, 1969, Diane Crump became the first woman to ride in a professional race. She rode at Florida's Hialeah Park. Some of the male jockeys refused to race against a woman. But despite the controversy, Crump managed to finish 10th in a field of 12.

Kusner and Crump had broken new ground. But that didn't cause a dramatic increase in the number of women who decided to become jockeys. It wasn't until 1972 that a female jockey received national attention.

That's when Robyn Smith began winning some pretty big races. *Sports Illustrated* magazine ran a cover story on her. The story described how badly Smith was treated because she was still the only woman rider at most tracks.

On March 1, 1973, Smith became the first woman to win an important stakes race. She won the Paumonok Handicap at Aqueduct Raceway in New York. It was a big step for women. But Smith married actor Fred Astaire and retired before really becoming a top jockey.

By 1979, there were only a few women jockeys. None of them had been good enough to make the jump into the top group. But this didn't bother Julie. She wasn't thinking about being a female jockey. She just wanted to be a jockey.

Only a few women jockeys, like Robyn Smith, had broken into professional racing before Julie. Here's Smith in a 1973 race in Arcadia, California.

"You don't think in terms of male and female when you're young," she said. "You just do what you like because you have a passion and desire for it."

So she started her journey. The next summer, in 1980, she began riding as an amateur at the half-mile state fair tracks in Michigan. That was just to gain experience. Julie learned how to break from the starting gate and how to position herself and her horse in the pack. She was still not a jockey, but she was practicing how to be one.

That December, Julie decided to make a big change. She left high school in her senior year and moved to Florida, where her grandmother lived. In Florida, Julie would be in a warm climate all year round. She could work toward becoming an apprentice jockey. That way she could continue the long learning process.

Shortly afterward, Julie Krone met Julie Snellings. Krone was working as an exercise rider at Tampa Bay Downs. Snellings was a steward's secretary. Racing stewards are like judges who watch the race to see if there are any fouls. If there are, they can disqualify the rider and his or her horse from the race. Snellings had seen Krone ride and decided to offer the 17-year-old some advice.

Young Julie didn't feel she should have to take advice from a secretary. "If you're so smart, how come you're not riding?" she asked. Julie never forgot what happened next.

"Julie [Snellings] rolled out from behind her desk in her wheelchair," Krone said later. "I wanted to crawl into a hole."

Julie Snellings had once been a jockey. In 1977, she was thrown during a race at Delaware Park.

"My horse landed on top of me and broke my back, also damaging my spine," Snellings explained. "I was paralyzed instantly."

In spite of their awkward beginning, the two women became good friends. Snellings had been on her way to becoming a fine rider when she was injured. Julie Krone was more than willing to listen to Julie Snellings's advice. Julie Snellings was more than willing to take the younger girl under her wing. "She had great talent. You could see that right away," Snellings said. "And she was different than I was. The trainers used to complain I was too ladylike a rider. But Julie was tough."

Julie learned fast. No one questioned her ability to ride. At 100 pounds, she easily handled horses that weighed well over 1,000 pounds. Julie was also absolutely fearless. She was never afraid of a challenge.

Finally, in January 1981, Julie became a full-fledged apprentice rider. Because apprentice jockeys are still learning, they can only ride in less important races. Julie's first mount as an apprentice came on January 30, in the third race at Florida's Tampa Bay Downs Race Track. The horse was named Tiny Star. Julie rode him to a second-place finish.

Julie wins her first race on February 12, 1981, on Lord Farkle at Tampa Bay Downs in Florida.

She kept working to ride that first winner. Then, on February 12, Julie was on a horse named Lord Farkle. It was the 11th race at Tampa Bay Downs. Julie suddenly found herself out in front. As the horses came down the homestretch, she stayed in front.

"The whole way down the stretch I kept waiting for somebody to pass me," Julie said.

It didn't happen. Julie and Lord Farkle crossed the finish line in front. At 17, Julie Krone had won her first race. Full of confidence, she was ready to compete against anyone. Julie was ready to become the best jockey she could be.

Chapter 4

Gaining Respect

Sometimes all it takes is a victory. Once Julie got a taste of the winner's circle, she wanted more. Shortly after her first victory on Lord Farkle, she began to ride for a top trainer named Bud Delp.

During the fall and winter of 1981, Julie rode Delp's horses. She rode them at both Pimlico Race Course in Maryland and at Delaware Park in Delaware. During these sessions, she brought home more than 100 winners.

Julie began riding and winning regularly in Atlantic City, New Jersey. She wasn't in the big races, but was among the top riders in Atlantic City almost immediately. She was gaining success by combining her talent with hard work.

It seemed as if Julie never stopped. Her day began by working out and galloping horses from 6 to 9 A.M. After that, she raced all afternoon at one track, then in the evenings drove to another track in Atlantic City. There, she raced from 7:30 to midnight.

It was an exhausting schedule. But Julie just loved to ride. She was also learning from famous jockeys like Angel Cordero, Jr. When he showed up for a big race, Julie asked him to watch her ride. She also studied the way Cordero handled a horse.

Julie's hard work was paying off. She became the leading rider in terms of winners at Atlantic City in both 1982 and 1983. Julie still wasn't riding in major races. But she was piling up the wins and getting more respect within the racing community.

In many of Julie's early races, the riders were usually instructed to stay close to the rail. The trainers didn't want the jockeys swinging wide. A horse running wide has to cover a greater distance than a horse that stays near the rail. Julie became very good at staying close to the rail. She had a reputation for being fearless about going through on the inside.

Good jockeys also need to adapt to each horse. They must use their hands, voice, seat, and legs to calm a nervous horse or to get a laid-back one to run faster. Julie was also good at this.

Competing in the big time wasn't easy. But Julie wasn't letting anything slow her down. In 1984, she continued to pile up winnings. Then, on August 25, 1985, Julie reached a real milestone.

Riding at Monmouth Park in New Jersey, Julie recorded her 1,000th victory. She had done this in a little over four years. That's top riding in any league. Her abilities were being noticed by even more people, including her peers.

Retired jockey Willie Shoemaker has won more races than any other jockey. He saw a special talent in Julie.

"Some jockeys have a kind of sixth sense," Shoemaker said. "You're communicating with the horse through the reins, and he can tell that you like him, and he likes you, and you both know it. I think you're born with that. Not all jockeys have it. Julie does."

Even with this sixth sense, Julie always studied hard. She wanted to know all she could about every horse she rode. Julie also wanted to know about the other horses in the race. If a horse ran a certain way, Julie wanted to know it.

Julie kept notes about the other horses and studied the Daily Racing Form. That way, she knew which horses liked to run in front. She also knew which ones liked to come from behind and which horses liked to stay on the rail.

More people were beginning to compliment Julie. One of them was Steven Crist, the racing columnist for *The New York Times*. Crist called Julie the best woman jockey he'd ever seen.

But it still wasn't an easy road for Julie. Some people still felt that a woman shouldn't be competing in what had always been a man's world. Julie still heard remarks from the stands. It was especially bad when she didn't win.

She also felt she had to stand up for her rights. An incident in July 1986 received national attention. Julie was in the lead in another close race at Monmouth Park. Jockey Miguel Rujano from Panama was riding the second-place horse. Down the homestretch, he tried to pass her. But Rujano couldn't get by Julie's horse. Julie went on to win the race easily.

That's when it happened. As the horses slowed to a trot, Rujano rode up alongside Julie. Next, he hit her in the head with his whip. At first, Julie ignored the blow. She simply followed the rules and went to the post-race weigh in.

After Julie stepped off the scales, she had some photos taken. Suddenly, she noticed her ear was bleeding. Someone heard her say, "Excuse me, I have to go hit someone."

Sure enough, Julie walked up to Rujano and punched him with her fist. Some observers said Rujano tried to punch Julie back. Rujano said that he did not try to hit Julie. But he did push her into a nearby swimming pool. When Julie stepped out, she picked up a deck chair and threw it at him. Bystanders finally broke up the fight.

Afterward, Julie did not want to talk about the incident. She wasn't happy about it. Rujano claimed that Julie had fouled him when he tried to pass her. He said he was trying to hit Julie's horse, not Julie.

Both riders were fined. Rujano was also suspended for five days. Richard Lawrenson was the track steward that day. He saw the incident differently.

"The guys try to intimidate women jockeys," Lawrenson said. "But Julie let them know she's not going to tolerate foolishness. She's also earned their respect as a rider."

That part was true. The little fight with Rujano was one of the last incidents of that kind Julie had to face.

Chapter 5

Top
Jockey

By 1987, Julie had put together a very impressive record. There was no denying her abilities now. She had become a top jockey. But some still felt that women jockeys were not strong enough to ride with men. Others disagreed. Flint Schulhofer spoke for many trainers when he described Julie's strength and determination as a rider.

"Julie's as strong as anybody," Schulhofer said. "She can get down and knuckle on a horse with the best of them."

All this was being proven by the numbers. In 1987, Julie was the sixth-leading rider in the nation, with 324 victories. She also became the first woman to win riding titles at major racetracks. She won at Monmouth Park with 130 wins. She also won at the Meadowlands in New Jersey with 124 victories.

There is an old saying in racing that you cannot get fast horses until you win races, and you cannot win races until you get fast horses. Julie was finally being given fast horses because of her hard work and winning record.

Here's Julie on July 14, 1987, covered with mud after a ride at Monmouth Park.

One racing writer said about Julie, "A big jockey will usually exercise a big horse for a big race. But she is always out there early, working the horses. And then she'll give the trainers and owners a move-by-move report."

Maybe Julie knew she would always have to work harder because she was a woman. But it was also part of her competitive nature to cover all the bases.

Julie was now racing against the best jockeys in the world. She knew she couldn't win if she made even a small mistake.

Julie first tackled the New York tracks in the winter of 1987–88. She made Aqueduct Raceway her winter base in December 1987. Her first day there Julie rode four winners. During the five-month Aqueduct winter season, she rode a total of 68 winners against the best riders in the world.

On March 6, 1988, Julie reached another major milestone. Still riding in New York, she drove home the 1,205th winner of her career. That victory pushed her past Patricia Cooksey as the female jockey with the most wins ever. Julie was only 24 years old.

Even now, a few trainers still called her a female jockey. She had a sharp answer for them.

"If you want a 'girl' jockey, get someone else," she said. "With me, you get reckless and aggressive."

Being aggressive can sometimes lead to injuries. On April 24, Julie was leading in another New York race. Jockey Randy Romero made his move between horses. Just as he moved past Julie, his mount cut in, and Julie's horse stumbled.

Julie bounced out of the saddle. She was able to hang onto the horse's neck for a few seconds before falling to the track. Then, the horse's hoof came pounding down on her shoulder. She lay on the track, still and stunned.

Julie is wearing a safety helmet. All jockeys must wear them during a race to protect themselves if they fall. Julie's injuries could have been worse on April 24, 1988, without a helmet.

The injuries could have been worse. Julie had torn muscles in her arm. She was only out a few weeks. But when she returned, she didn't get as many quality horses to ride. As a result, her first two weeks back showed only two winners in fifty tries.

That's how it is in racing. If you disappear for a while with an injury, you have to prove yourself all over again. At the end of May, Julie decided to return to New Jersey to race. But on her final day at Belmont, she had another spill. It left her with a concussion that kept her out three more days.

Still, Julie wound up the 1988 season as the fourth-best rider in the nation. She had 363 victories. Julie was also the top-money-winning female jockey for the third year in a row.

In 1986, her horses had earned $2.3 million. In 1987 they had earned $4.5 million. Now, in 1988, Julie had brought home winners to the tune of $7.7 million in purses. That showed she was getting better mounts and bigger races.

Julie was the leading rider at Monmouth Park and the Meadowlands Race Track once more. She also received the Big Sport of Turfdom Award for that year.

For most of 1989, Julie continued on target. She still wasn't given the very top riding assignments. But she was getting close to that goal. It was obvious that she was quickly becoming a star. It would have been even better had it not been for her worse fall yet.

On November 24, Julie fell off her horse at one of her favorite tracks, the Meadowlands. She badly fractured her left arm. A plate and seven screws had to be inserted so that it would heal properly. This injury finished her for the 1989 season and also for a good part of 1990.

Julie missed the final five weeks of the year. But she wound up the third-leading rider in the country, with 368 victories. Her total earnings hit the $8 million mark. But the arm took time to heal.

Back in action, Julie had to fight for good mounts once again. She returned to become the leading rider at the Meadowlands for the fourth straight year. But Julie had only $2.8 million in earnings in 1990. That was still the best among female jockeys, but it was her lowest total since 1986. The arm injury had kept her out of action for more than half the year.

Once again Julie was at a kind of crossroads. But she had fought and won against the odds before.

Chapter 6

Belmont Triumph

In 1991, Julie did a lot of riding around the New York area. She wanted better mounts and bigger races. An important goal was to ride in grade I stakes races. Grade I stakes are the top races, with the largest purses, or winning money. Julie also hoped to have a mount in one of the Triple Crown races. The first Triple Crown race is the Kentucky Derby. It is followed by the Preakness Stakes and then by the Belmont Stakes.

Julie soon began winning. She wasn't riding in as many races. But her winning races had bigger prizes.

One big race is the Withers Stakes. Julie won it on a horse named Subordinated Debt. Then in June 1991, she became the first woman ever to ride in the Belmont Stakes. Once again her horse was Subordinated Debt. Julie finished a disappointing ninth. But she proved again that she could compete with anyone in a big race.

Julie had another successful year in 1991. She was once again the top female rider in winnings, with $7.7 million in purses. Julie was also the

Before a race, the weight of each jockey is officially recorded. Julie is sitting next to a scale before the race on July 8, 1992.

second-leading rider at Saratoga Race Track in New York. She was just one victory behind the leader, Mike Smith.

In 1992, Julie continued on the fast track. She won more grade I stakes races and handicap races. Handicap races are for older horses. To make the race more even, the better horses carry more weight. Some of the big races Julie won were the Forego Handicap, the Lexington Handicap, the New York Handicap, the Pilgrim Stakes, the Red Smith Handicap, and the Tom Fool Stakes.

For the second year in a row, Julie was given a horse in the Belmont Stakes. This time she rode Colony

Light to a sixth-place finish. She was still the only woman ever to ride in one of the Triple Crown races.

In 1992 Julie won a career-high $9.1 million in purses. That was ninth best in the entire nation. She was the leading rider at Gulfstream Park in Florida. Julie also won the Belmont Spring Meet with 73 victories. She became New York's fourth-leading rider with 158 wins.

Julie was now a well-known sports celebrity. She had appeared on television talk shows. Many magazine stories were written about her. *Sports Illustrated* had already done a cover story on her in 1989. It described her as the best female jockey ever.

As 1993 began, fewer people were focusing on Julie as a female jockey. Now, there was little doubt that she was simply one of the best.

Julie racing on July 8, 1992. That season she won a career-high $9.1 million in earnings.

Julie truly loves horses. Here, one of the horses she rides, Wintertime Sport, tries to take away Julie's popsicle.

Julie had already won more than 2,500 races. Her career earnings were closing in on $50 million. Julie's share of the winnings enabled her to lead a very comfortable life. She owned a 10-acre farm with indoor riding facilities in Colts Neck, New Jersey. It was home, a place where she could relax.

But the place Julie still liked to be the most was on a fast horse in a big race. She was in the middle of another fine year in 1993, when trainer Flint

Schulhofer put her on a large horse named Colonial Affair for a race at Aqueduct Raceway on April 9.

Colonial Affair was a three-year-old. He had won just a single race in the four races he had run the year before. But Schulhofer was looking at having him run in the Belmont Stakes in June. Run at a one-and-one-half-mile distance, it is the longest of the Triple Crown races.

In the April race, Julie kept the big horse near the front. Then Colonial Affair exploded down the backstretch. He won the race by a huge margin. A month later, Julie and Colonial Affair won another race at Belmont Park. Then on May 23, they were entered in the Peter Pan Stakes at Belmont.

This time Julie took the lead early. But then another horse blew by her down the stretch and won by two lengths.

Julie and Schulhofer learned from that race. When she mounted Colonial Affair to run in the Belmont Stakes, everyone was ready. As Julie entered the starting gate, she thought about what Schulhofer had told her the night before.

"Some people say you can't win the big ones," he said. "Look at this as just another race. Let him relax the first part of it. Be patient. You can do it."

Julie rode the race of her life. Colonial Affair won in a race that wasn't even close. Julie had become the first woman to win the Belmont as well as a Triple Crown race.

After the race, former jockey George Martens said, "Beautiful job, Julie." She turned to him and asked, "How do you stop crying?"

"You don't," Martens answered.

Schulhofer couldn't have been happier. "Julie rode the horse to perfection," he said.

Later Julie called her parents. Her mother told Julie, "I'm on the ceiling. Come scrape me off."

As Julie left the jockey's room, she came across Ron Turcotte. He had been a top jockey and had ridden the great racehorse Secretariat to the Triple Crown in 1973. Some years later Turcotte had been paralyzed in a bad spill from a horse. He was now in a wheelchair. All jockeys know the risk they take.

But on this day Ron Turcotte wanted to share Julie's joy. "You're so happy you don't know where you're going, right?" he said to Julie.

"I'm delirious," she answered.

"You should be," Turcotte said. "You just rode yourself into the record book."

Chapter 7

Near Tragedy and the Battle to Come Back

Julie went right back to work. Soon after the Belmont, she headed to Saratoga for the racing season there. As usual, she was having a very successful run.

On August 20, Julie had a fantastic day, riding five winners. Once again, she showed the huge crowd that she had truly become a great rider. Then, ten days later, on August 30, Julie had a day that all jockeys dread.

She was riding Seattle Way in the third race. It was still early in the race. Jockey Filberto Leon was aboard Bejilla Lass and was boxed in. He tried to get his horse free. In doing so, Filberto's horse bumped Seattle Way.

Julie was knocked from her saddle. She spun around so that, for a split second, she was facing the horses behind her. Then she tumbled to the turf. A horse rode right over Julie, kicking her in the chest. A hush came over the crowd. Everyone knew that she had been badly hurt.

"I got hit in the heart," Julie remembered. "My arm was cut so that you could see the elbow socket.

My ankle hurt so bad I kept thinking, 'Pass out. Please, pass out!' But I didn't. For the first time I said to myself, 'This is dangerous!'"

As she lay there, she also thought, "What's wrong with you? What are you doing in this business?" But Julie was thankful for the pain. "It took my mind off that stuff."

Julie's ankle was smashed in 11 places. She also had a bruise to her heart. If she hadn't been wearing a protective vest, the kick to the chest might have killed her. At Saratoga Hospital, she lay in a bed in severe pain.

"The pain was so wicked I spent five hours just crying my eyes out," Julie said. Those around her said it was more like screaming. Nothing stopped the pain. The next day she was flown to Staten Island University Hospital in New York City.

Dr. Frank Ariosta, who is an orthopedic surgeon, operated on Julie's ankle. He had to insert two metal plates and 14 screws

Julie puts her arm around Dr. Frank Ariosta in the interview room at Belmont Park on May 24, 1994. He operated on her ankle after the racing accident that nearly killed her on August 30, 1993.

into the ankle. There were doubts whether Julie would ever race again. No one even knew how well she would be able to walk.

In the hospital, Julie realized how many friends and fans she had. Many of her fellow jockeys visited her. She received letters from all around the country.

In the hospital, Julie also had a chance to reflect on her life. "My lifeline was racing and winning," she said. "Then, suddenly, it became my friends and fans. Thinking you don't need anyone, that's not real life."

But Julie also was already thinking about coming back. The target date was July 1, 1994. That would mean ten months away from what she loved the most—racing and competing.

"I'm going to have to prove myself all over again," she said. "I'm sure there will be people thinking, 'Oh, she's going to be scared now.'"

Julie planned to be the same Julie Krone, aggressive and fearless. But getting the ankle back in shape wasn't easy.

There were nights when Julie would awaken and forget she had a shattered ankle. She would step out of bed and fall to the floor. The ankle couldn't support her weight. Rehabilitation was difficult and painful. It had to be done every day. A lesser person might have quit. But Julie thought of just one thing. She had to get back up on a horse and race again.

Julie's grit and work ethic triumphed. Her return to racing was announced for May 25, 1994, at Belmont Park. That was more than a month ahead of her targeted comeback date.

Julie's comeback race drew great fanfare. Reporters flocked to see her at the track. They asked Julie about her ankle and her feelings.

"Coming back to the races doesn't feel like winning a Triple Crown race," she told them.

Julie kisses a small friend and neighbor after she rides Baypark to a third-place finish in the eighth race at New York's Belmont Park on May 25, 1994.

"Nothing can top that. But coming back from a career-threatening injury, it makes you more thankful just to be able to ride again. And I know I still have the passion for riding and getting into the winner's circle again."

Julie made her debut on Baypark in the fourth race. She made a solid run, finishing third. Then, Julie rode a horse named Life Boat. They came home a disappointing eighth. The finish wasn't what Julie wanted. But the fact that she was racing again was what counted.

Julie is riding Life Boat on May 25, 1994, at Belmont. It's her first race after her 1993 racing accident at Saratoga.

Julie still couldn't walk very well or for very long. The pins and plates remained in her ankle. They would come out in about six months.

Julie raced from May 25 to November 9. During that time, she rode 101 winners. Julie was beginning to look as good as ever. Then, on November 11, she had surgery for the removal of the plates and pins. More rehabilitation followed.

The surgery kept Julie out until January 4, 1995. Her return was at Gulfstream Park in Florida. That day she was scheduled for five races.

Julie is ready for the opening day of the racing season at Florida's Gulfstream Park on January 4, 1995. She is returning to racing after the plates and pins in her ankle were removed.

"Taking so much time away has slowed me down so much," Julie said. "Now we have to almost start over again."

That day Julie won the Breeders' Cup Spectacular Bid Stakes on Mr. Greeley. It was a first step. But Julie knew she was no longer a hot jockey.

Just ten days after her return, Julie was injured again. She was riding a horse named Saratoga Source at Gulfstream Park. They were running last, out of heavy traffic. Saratoga Source went down with a broken right foreleg. Julie was thrown into the air, and the horse rolled over her. It was another frightening moment.

Saratoga Source was badly injured and had to be destroyed. Julie was luckier. She had a broken finger on her left hand. A pin had to be inserted there.

This time Julie was supposed to be out until mid-March 1995. She would have to come back once again.

"I'm okay," Julie said afterward. "My ankle hurts a bit, but it will be all right. I'm just having a tough time holding the telephone."

Such is the life of a jockey. But for Julie Krone, it's been even more than that. First, she had to overcome being a woman in what had been a man's world. Julie did that better than any other female jockey ever had.

Then there were the injuries. The worst was her near-fatal spill in 1993. Now the trick seems to be staying healthy. Julie will be 32 years old in 1995. This is not old for a jockey. Some jockeys race right into their fifties. The only question is whether her body can hold up. There are already signs of traumatic arthritis that won't go away in her bad ankle.

But Julie has already ridden in more than 16,000 races, winning nearly 3,000 of them. She has more than $54 million in career earnings. She won the Women's Sports Foundation Award as Female Athlete of the Year in 1993. That same year, Julie was named one of *Glamour* magazine's ten Women of the Year.

With all that success, why would she want to continue in such a dangerous sport? Perhaps it is a combination of her love of horses and her desire to compete. Julie has been described as one of the most competitive athletes in the world. She even admits that her competitiveness is what drives her.

"I think fear gets replaced by competitiveness," she has said. "I'm not here just in body. I'm here in body and soul." It sounds as if Julie Krone will be there for a long time to come.

Julie Krone's
Career Highlights

1987   First woman to win riding titles at major racetracks with victories at Monmouth Park (130 wins) and the Meadowlands (124 wins).

Rode six winners at Monmouth Park, equaling the track record for a single day, on August 19.

Equaled the Meadowlands record of five wins on a single day in October.

Became the only woman jockey to win four races in New York in one day, at Aqueduct on December 13.

1988   Became the female rider with the most all-time wins on March 6 with win number 1,205.

1991   Became the first woman to ride in a Triple Crown race when she rode Subordinated Debt in the Belmont Stakes.

1993   Became the only woman to win a Triple Crown race when she rode Colonial Affair to victory in the Belmont Stakes in June.

Became the third jockey in history to win five races in one day at Saratoga on August 20 and the first to do it in 20 years.

1994   Is the all-time leader in wins, with 2,861, and in earnings, with $57,561,127, for a female jockey.

Julie Krone's
Racing Record

Year	Races	1st	2nd	3rd
1981	747	124	106	120
1982	1,049	155	150	146
1983	1,024	151	140	138
1984	801	108	95	121
1985	1,041	106	140	119
1986	1,442	199	208	182
1987	1,698	324	270	241
1988	1,958	363	331	273
1989	1,673	368	287	235
1990	634	142	120	81
1991	1,414	230	229	188
1992	1,445	278	243	190
1993	1,012	212	171	136
1994	571	101	84	80
Totals	16,509	2,861	2,574	2,250

Julie Krone's
Career Earnings

Year	Races in the Money*	Earnings
1981	350	$ 796,773
1982	451	$ 1,238,161
1983	429	$ 1,095,662
1984	324	$ 788,412
1985	365	$ 1,060,352
1986	589	$ 2,357,136
1987	835	$ 4,522,191
1988	967	$ 7,770,314
1989	890	$ 8,031,445
1990	343	$ 2,577,727
1991	647	$ 7,748,007
1992	711	$ 9,191,148
1993	519	$ 6,415,462
1994	265	$ 3,968,337
Totals	7,685	$57,561,127

*"In the money" means finishing first, second, or third.

Further Reading

Callahan, Dorothy M. *Julie Krone: A Winning Jockey.* New York: Macmillan Child Group, 1990.

Ettinger, Tom, and Jaspersohn, Bill. *My Riding Book: A Write-In-Me Book for Young Readers.* New York: HarperCollins, 1993.

Harns, Jack. *The Kentucky Derby.* Mankato, MN: Creative Education, 1990.

Kidd, Jane. *Learning to Ride.* New York: Howell Books, 1993.

Index

Index cont.

The World of
CROSSFIT

DANCE & FITNESS
TRENDS

Pete
DiPrimio

Mitchell Lane
PUBLISHERS

P.O. Box 196
Hockessin, DE 19707

Mitchell Lane
PUBLISHERS

African Dance Trends
Get Fit with Video Workouts
Line Dances Around the World
Trends in Hip-Hop Dance
Trends in Martial Arts
The World of CrossFit
Yoga Fitness
Zumba Fitness

PUBLISHER'S NOTE: The facts in this book have been thoroughly researched. Documentation of such research can be found on page 44. While every possible effort has been made to ensure accuracy, the publisher will not assume liability for damages caused by inaccuracies in the data, and makes no warranty on the accuracy of the information contained herein.

The Internet sites referenced herein were active as of the publication date. Due to the fleeting nature of some web sites, we cannot guarantee that they will all be active when you are reading this book.

Printing 1 2 3 4 5 6 7 8 9

Library of Congress
Cataloging-in-Publication Data FORTHCOMING

DiPrimio, Pete.
 The world of CrossFit / by Pete DiPrimio.
   pages cm. — (Dance and fitness trends)
 Includes bibliographical references and index.
 ISBN 978-1-61228-552-8 (library bound)
 1. Physical education and training—Juvenile literature. 2. Physical fitness—Juvenile literature. 3. Exercise—Juvenile literature. 4. CrossFit, Inc.—Juvenile literature. I. Title.
 GV711.5.D57 2014
 613.7—dc23
                                          2014006931

eBook ISBN: 9781612285924

Contents

Introduction

CrossFit has a clown for a mascot, but it's no joke.

CrossFit emphasizes back-to-the-basics training with constantly changing routines called Workouts of the Day (WODs in CrossFit talk). The philosophy of CrossFit is that you can get in better shape with short, intense workouts. You just need some clothes and shoes to work out in, and a willingness to push yourself harder than you thought possible.

Does it work?

"I'd never had muscles," says Lee Stewart, a certified CrossFit instructor and forty-something mother of four from Indiana. "With CrossFit, I got them. My husband Jim said, 'You've never looked like an athlete. Now, you do.'"

CrossFit works for athletes (triathlon competitors often use it as part of their training) and for those who just want to stay in shape.

CrossFit is for people of all ages. CrossFit gyms (called "boxes") can have members ranging from four years old to older than seventy. The workout emphasizes "functional movement," which means working the muscle in a way you would in real life—building muscle while doing something with that muscle.

"I could do bicep curls until I'm blue in the face," says Indianapolis television anchor and fitness enthusiast Lauren Lowrey, "but when I'm using my biceps in real life, I'm never just standing there curling my arms. Usually, I'm using my biceps to lift a piece of furniture and move it. In those situations, I'm using my lower body while stabilizing my core and dealing with a racing heart."

CrossFit training for kids is not the same as it is for adults. The focus is less on intensity and more on fun and fundamentals.

"We'll often coach them to do their best work, but not their fastest, hardest work," Jenna Innis Tieman says. She co-owns Hoosier CrossFit in Bloomington, Indiana. "Kids tend to cut corners and get sloppy in competitive situations. We want to help them learn how to move well, and then move well fast."

Forget no pain, no gain, at least when it comes to motivating teenagers. So how do CrossFit instructors get them to stay with it? By understanding "how to push their buttons," Lee Stewart says. She should know. She trained both of her teenage sons.

"It has to be fun and they have to learn the proper movements," she says.

"You're coaching with a mental intensity to it that can be unpleasant. It's like, 'Oh my God, this is going to suck!' You have to push yourself every time. Kids don't always want that."

CrossFit is a group workout. There are no earphones or iPods or doing your own thing. You know your coaches and other members by name. Coaches cheer you on when you struggle and when you set personal records. Members push and encourage each other. This is a commitment and not a fad, which means you do it several times a week, every week. Many people keep a journal of their workouts to see how much they've improved.

How hard is CrossFit? Its mascot clown is called Pukie (as in working so hard you get sick) for a reason.

What is that reason?

Is it really for kids?

Let's take a look.

CrossFit often involves running, either for short or long distances. It can help athletes improve in track as well as other sports.

Chapter 1
Hurting So Good

Sarah Hoffman hurt so good. She didn't fear the blood and pain. The goal was so close; the achievement was so personal.

Sarah had one hundred pull-ups to do: eighty-five down, fifteen to go in this Workout of the Day. And if her hands looked like they'd been chewed by an aggressive squirrel, big deal. If she knew things like holding a hair brush would be out of the question for the next week, well, so what?

Quit?

No way.

Music blared loud and fast at Bloomington CrossFit in Indiana. It always did when Carl, a certified CrossFit trainer, ran the high-energy show.

Sarah was a seventeen-year-old senior at Bloomington South High School in the spring of 2013. She was a soccer and track star who hoped that a big finish to her high school track career would earn her a college scholarship. She planned to attend Denison University, a small college near Columbus, Ohio.

She ran the 400 meters for Bloomington South and wanted to break 60 seconds. Her friend Elliott, a hockey and lacrosse player, had shown impressive speed and strength gains with CrossFit. He told Sarah that the increasingly popular system combines weightlifting, gymnastics, body weight exercises, and aerobic exercises like sprints, with some giant tire flipping thrown in. She decided to try it.

It was a big commitment. Sarah would go to 5:00 a.m. CrossFit workouts before school, then to track practice after school. It was tough—and worth it. She ran a 61.9 second 400, then a 61.2, then 60.4.

"Then I got to 60.02, which was the worst," she says. She had been so close, but didn't quite break 60 seconds.

Finally, at the Indiana state championships for track, as a member of Bloomington South's relay team, she ran 400 meters in 59.9 seconds. "CrossFit training really helped," she says.

But before Sarah reached her goal in track, she was at Bloomington CrossFit, going for one hundred pull-ups.

Sarah couldn't do unassisted pull-ups, so a strong elastic band was attached to the bar that helped give her a boost. She gripped the bar on the top of a squat rack, stood on the elastic band, and started doing pull-ups along with other WOD participants.

After every minute Carl would shout, "Minute!" Sarah would stop doing pull-ups, get off the rack and do three burpees, then start doing pull-ups again.

"I was pumping out pull-ups no problem at the beginning," she says, "but after a while my arms started to feel like Jell-O. I had to talk to myself just to keep moving."

The skin around the palms of her hands began to blister and tear.

"I didn't realize it until I got to eighty-five pull-ups, and at that point, you have fifteen to go. Why not finish?"

So Sarah did, completing one hundred pull-ups, plus thirty-three burpees, in just over eleven minutes.

Her hands were a mess. Later, after another tough WOD tore up her hands again, her mother made her wear gloves.

"I used the gloves . . . half the time," Sarah says. "They get in the way a lot, but on bar-heavy days, I know they're better than bleeding hands."

Sarah continued doing CrossFit in the summer of 2013 to prepare for her freshman season at Denison. She said the benefits went beyond conditioning.

"CrossFit produces a sense of community," she says. "There can be friendly competition as far as who can do the most

In many ways, Sarah Hoffman was a typical high school senior. But with the help of CrossFit, she was able to reach her athletic goals. More importantly, her success in track helped her to attend the college of her choice.

push-ups, but later they're pushing you to do your best. People are encouraging whether you're lifting 25 pounds or 125."

CrossFit is not for those seeking the easy road to fitness, which might be why one WOD is called "Fight Gone Bad." WODs can be so hard that sometimes people throw up (think Pukie the Clown). As your fitness improves, workouts get harder, and satisfaction increases.

In CrossFit, form is as important as effort. California's Margaret Hodel powers through a second round of pull-ups, making sure her chin clears the bar, during a competition honoring fallen US soldiers.

CrossFit WODs sometimes include AMRAPs: As Many Rounds As Possible. So, in a twenty-minute period, you might do as many pull-ups, kettlebell swings, and other exercises as you can.

Some people think this is great. Others think it's asking for injury.

"That's one reason why it can be miserable," Lee Stewart says. "You go as hard as you can. It's all about keeping moving. You can rest when it's over."

And then, for those who can take it, it hurts so good.

"Being pushed farther than you thought you could go is a great feeling," Sarah says.

WODs to Try

CrossFit targets these key physical skills: **cardiovascular/respiratory endurance, stamina, strength, flexibility, power, speed, coordination, agility, balance, and accuracy.** To get an idea of how tough a CrossFit workout can be, take a look at a couple of examples:

Workout of the Day (WOD) Example 1:
   400m Run
   Then, 3 rounds of:
   21 Pull-Ups
   15 Box Jumps
   15 Wall Balls
   400m Run

WOD Example 2:
   27 Thrusters
   4 Legless rope climbs
   21 Thrusters
   3 Legless rope climbs
   15 Thrusters
   2 Legless rope climbs
   9 Thrusters
   1 Legless rope climbs

See Glossary of Exercises for descriptions of each exercise. Never attempt exercises without supervision from a trained coach.

Dance 11 Fitness

Greg Glassman spreads the CrossFit word. Under his direction, CrossFit has gone from a California fad to a worldwide fitness success. His message is clear—CrossFit is not for everyone, just the tough and tough-minded.

Chapter 2
The Beginning

Greg Glassman had an idea. He was a former gymnast who pushed himself hard in workouts he designed. He did away with fancy, expensive equipment and distracting mirrors in order to stick with the basics. The key—were you tough enough to do them?

In 1974, Glassman began training others in Southern California. By 1995, he had opened the first CrossFit gym in Santa Cruz, and was training the local police department. People talked about his grueling workouts. He began posting his WOD online every day. People talked some more.

It took ten years for the idea to catch on nationally, but once it did, it was here to stay. There were eighteen affiliated gyms in 2005. By 2010, there were almost 1,700. Three years later, there were more than 10,000.

Glassman is a colorful guy, a tough guy, a guy who does not back down from what he believes, and a guy who is not afraid to shake things up. For example, some people think that Pukie the Clown sends a bad message. They say he encourages participants to push their bodies too far. But that didn't stop Glassman from putting an image of the clown on a company plane. He says it's funny.

Sometimes he says things that upset people. For instance, "[CrossFit] can kill you. I've always been completely honest about that."

But then he also says, "We're changing the world. We're doing all the right things for all the right people for all the right reasons. And it's a load of fun."

CrossFit is so effective, even US Marines use it. Here, Sergeant Julio C. Gonzalez leads a dozen recruits through a three-day CrossFit training seminar in Minneapolis. The goal is to improve the recruits' fitness before they join the Marines.

Fun comes with nine basic moves divided into three groups of three:

1) Air squat, front squat, and overhead squat
2) Shoulder press, push press, and push jerk
3) Deadlift, sumo deadlift high pull, and medicine ball clean

The second and third moves in each group build upon the basics of the first move in the group.

Then there are eleven specialty training courses: defense, endurance, football, gymnastics, kettlebell, mobility, weightlifting, powerlifting, row, striking, and strongman.

WODS are timed. There's often a friendly competitiveness to the workouts, which encourages participants to do their best. People try to finish the workout as quickly as possible, while still maintaining good form in every exercise.

"The key is intensity," instructor Lee Stewart says. "The longer a workout goes, the less you are able to maintain high intensity. Most WODS are in the ten- to twenty-five-minute range."

Some CrossFit workouts have names. For instance, there is Eva, which has five rounds. Each round consists of an 800-meter run, thirty kettlebell swings, and thirty pull-ups.

A really fit person might finish Eva in thirty-five minutes or even less. An average CrossFit participant could get through this workout in about forty-five minutes. And for some, it can take fifty-five minutes or longer.

Then there's Murph, which is named after Lieutenant Michael Murphy, a Navy SEAL who was killed in Afghanistan. It consists of a one-mile run, one hundred pull-ups, two hundred push-ups, three hundred squats, and another one-mile run. You can divide the workout into sets of, say, five pull-ups, ten push-ups, and fifteen squats, and do it twenty times. While a beginner could take over an hour to finish Murph, the most athletic CrossFitters can complete it in under thirty minutes.

CrossFit can be done anytime, anywhere. US Army Major Eric Wieland of Iowa led a round of push-ups during a "Murph" CrossFit workout at an Afghanistan military base.

The action was non-stop at the 2012 Reebok CrossFit Games. Competitors are closely watched by judges to make sure they do each event correctly and completely.

Other workouts include more cardiovascular exercises. Small, named after Army Staff Sergeant Marc Small, consists of three rounds of: rowing 1,000 meters on a machine, fifty burpees, fifty box jumps, and running 800 meters.

Then there are the CrossFit Games. These competitions are designed to identify the fittest men and women, not just in the United States, but in the world.

Glassman is not shy about the benefits of training with CrossFit.

"The strength and value of CrossFit lies entirely within our total dominance of other athletes," he said. "This is a truth that cannot be divined through debate, only competition."

In other words, may the best man and woman win.

Sometimes really intense workouts can cause rhabdomyolysis, a very rare but serious condition that comes from a massive breakdown of muscle cells. This can result in damage to the kidneys as well.

If pushed to the limit and beyond, muscle cells die, sending protein into the blood stream. The protein winds up in the kidneys, which eliminate it from the body. But too much protein can overload and damage the kidneys. Meanwhile, the damaged muscles start to swell. The longer rhabdomyolysis is left untreated, the worse the complications can be. In some cases, it can result in the loss of a limb. Others may require surgery to relieve the pressure and swelling around the muscle.

"If you look at the statistics, it's very rare," Lee Stewart says. "Most boxes are trained to be aware of it. You usually have small classes, with ten to twelve participants. The coaches know what you can do and how hard you work. They push you, but they monitor and watch your form."

Jenna Innis Tieman, a certified CrossFit instructor and co-owner of Hoosier CrossFit in Indiana says they've "never had a case of it." They make sure all members are eased into training with a beginning twelve-class program.

"If somebody wants to join our gym and get right into group classes, they might not fit our style because we're protecting them. We protect them from that intensity and competitive nature when it's premature. We slow them down and make them focus on movement, not intensity.

"For those who don't accept that, for coaches who want people to get crazy and load up heavy, you'll see rhabdomyolysis and injuries."

CrossFit is tough, but that doesn't mean kids can't do it. West Virginia trainer Shanna Thompson shows six-year-old Campion Carrico how to push a sled across a gym floor.

Chapter 3
Kids' Way

Keeran and Ahna bear crawl across a dark padded floor at the Hoosier CrossFit box in Indiana. The brother and sister stop, listen to instructor Heather Ross, and do it again, then crawl under a bench, and jump over a box.

In a moment, they will climb rope, pulling themselves from the floor to a standing position. Then they will do a series of ten-yard sprints. After that, they will do push-ups.

Keeran is eight years old and Ahna is eleven. And they go hard. They are slender and quick, and follow instructions easily. On the side, their mother stretches to prepare for her own upcoming workout.

Along the way, Heather encourages with smiles and congratulates with high fives. There are games like 'Simon Says' with fitness movements, with the loser doing five squats. This is fun along with fitness. In twenty minutes or so, they are done. Around them, twenty-two adults have gathered for their own, more intense session.

Outside it is a brutally cold, brilliantly sunny winter day. A strong wind makes the twenty-eight-degree temperatures feel ten degrees colder. Inside this 5,700-square-foot open facility, there is plenty of room to generate your own heat.

There are twelve rowing machines and twelve sets of squat racks. Five pieces of equipment called glute-ham developers (GHDs) line a far wall. They are designed to work the gluteal muscles (buttocks), hamstrings (backs of legs), and core. Wooden boxes of various heights are used to jump up on, and then off. Giant truck tires are lying around, waiting to be

Weightlifting is part of the CrossFit challenge. It was no problem for twelve-year-old Hannah Wessling during a competition that involved thirty different lifts.

flipped. There are bars and weights ready for participants to perform Olympic-style weightlifting.

Twelve rings hang from the ceiling, as if set up for a gymnastics meet. They are very popular. Next to them are heavy ropes meant to be climbed.

And so they will be.

Watching is Jenna Innis Tieman, the co-owner of Hoosier CrossFit. She is a dark-haired, fit woman who looks you in the eye when talking. She is passionate about CrossFit and serious about its benefits, when done properly.

"It's a sport and we respect the sport," she says. "Let's have fun, but let's do it the right way."

Fun can mean relay races or other games, "So kids end their sessions on a good note," Jenna says. Kids' sessions are not meant to be hyperintense the way they can be for adults. She compares her training method to shaping food like cute animals so kids will want to eat it.

"Traditional workouts are hidden," she says, "like hiding zucchini in their burgers."

CrossFit for kids is designed to make them feel good, and not to hurt. "We want to keep them constantly moving and engaged," Jenna says. "It's different from adult classes where you're there to achieve a certain level of flexibility, or to see how great you can be in a single workout.

"With kids, we teach the deadlift because it's functional, but we don't max them out to see how much weight they can lift."

CrossFit is a way to stay healthy while competing. Some school systems across the country have incorporated CrossFit into their school curricula to encourage and develop fitness.

At Hoosier CrossFit, participants are divided into small groups. Overall membership approaches two hundred people, with ages ranging from four to sixty-seven.

Jenna pushes the fundamentals, making sure each exercise is done right. When you squat, "it's hips below the knee level

Jenna Innis Tieman's passion for CrossFit led her to become a coach and co-owner of Hoosier CrossFit. She teaches her students—young and old—to focus on doing exercises the right way, even if that means doing fewer reps than the person next to them.

because it's functional," she says. "You should be comfortable in that position." When you do a push-up, "your body touches the ground" when you go down and "your arms fully lock out" when you push yourself up.

Hoosier CrossFit has the feel of a competitive sports environment. Students listen to instructors as if they are coaches, because that's what they are. This doesn't mean that kids are so focused on out-doing the participant next to them that they cheat by not going all the way down on a push-up. The idea is that it's better to do five the right way than to do ten halfway.

All eyes were on these CrossFit instructors as they showed how to do a squat correctly. This CrossFit training session, held at an Iraq military base, leads to certification as a CrossFit coach. After completing their training, these students can begin training others in group classes.

"When kids are comparing each other and competing, they might end up wanting to cut corners so they can be winners," Jenna says. "Our program is fun with a competitive nature, but it requires accountability. They're not being honest when they cut corners."

Jenna began CrossFit as a way to lose weight after gaining thirty pounds in college. Her boyfriend, Shaun, who eventually became her husband, introduced her to CrossFit, and she loved it. She passed on a teaching career to become a CrossFit instructor and business owner.

So how does a person become a certified coach? The Level 1 Certificate Course runs for two days and costs $1,000. Seminars are held throughout the country and often sell out. With a Level 1 Certification, a trainer can begin teaching CrossFit group classes. Then there's a Coach's Prep Course, which builds on the skills that were learned in Level 1. That costs an additional $1,000. CrossFit recommends that coaches have at least six months' experience training with CrossFit methods before taking this intermediate-level course. CrossFit also offers training for coaches seeking to specialize in areas such as defense, endurance, CrossFit for kids, weightlifting, kettlebells, and more.

Full-time trainers who have a large number of members in their classes might make $60,000 a year. Some also sell books, DVDs, and equipment for extra income. Those coaches with enough clients can make $100,000 a year or more in some areas.

While the money is important, it's the passion and results that makes it worthwhile. "What matters is how [members] respect each other at the end of our sessions," Jenna says, "and how you can work harder to strengthen your weaknesses if you care about your progress."

The Paleo Diet

Is eating like a caveman or cavewoman good for you?

CrossFit trainers say yes, which is why a lot of them encourage people to use the Paleo Diet to complement their training.

The Paleo Diet attempts to replicate the diet of people in the Paleolithic era, which ended about ten thousand years ago. It was only after the end of this era that people began farming extensively.

Foods you can eat while on this diet include fresh meats from grass-fed animals. This includes beef, pork, lamb, poultry, and even game meat such as elk and deer. The diet also allows fish and seafood, fresh fruits, vegetables, seeds, nuts, eggs, and healthy oils such as olive, coconut, avocado, macadamia, walnut, and flaxseed.

People on the Paleo Diet don't eat dairy products, grains, legumes, or refined sugar. They also can't have processed foods such as canned foods, chips, pretzels, sugary breakfast cereals, cookies, hot dogs, sausage, and packaged lunch meats. These processed foods often have lots of calories, saturated fats, and sodium.

Sarah Hoffman went on the Paleo Diet briefly to help clean out her system after her migraine headaches were eventually traced to a gluten intolerance. She finally returned to a more normal diet.

"I did feel more awake and focused during the day while on the Paleo Diet, but it made it harder to do things like grab a coffee with friends since the coffee had to be black or with natural almond milk," she says.

Lee Stewart tried the Paleo diet for Lent, a six-week period of sacrifice which leads up to Easter.

"It's amazing how good you feel," she says. "You cut out all processed food. You don't eat sugar. I have my cheats—I like to have chocolate squares—but the more you stray, the worse you feel."

Despite being a mother of four children, Lee Stewart makes time to stay in shape with CrossFit. As a certified coach, she helps others do the same.

Chapter 4
No Shortcuts

Leonie Stewart (she prefers Lee) is the kind of mom you'd want to have if mom was, well, Wonder Woman.

She is lean and fit and fun. She smiles often, trains hard, and makes no excuses, which is what you'd expect from a certified CrossFit instructor. Fitness comes with a price she's willing to pay, and that's just as true for her kids as it is for herself.

"It's about raising kids to value physical fitness," she says, "so that whatever life throws at you, you can perform decently."

Lee took up CrossFit while she, her husband Jim, and their four children lived in Okinawa, Japan. He was in the Navy, and Okinawa was one of fifteen places they've lived since they met as Oregon State University students. Their latest stop—Bloomington, Indiana.

Lee had given birth to two children in her mid-twenties and two more in her thirties. She decided it was time to get in shape.

"To try losing weight after thirty is hard," she says. But Lee had another motivation—she wanted to "look nice in a dress."

CrossFit delivered.

"I love how it makes me feel. I feel very empowered when I do the WODs. It's hard to explain. It doesn't make a lot of sense. You do things you didn't think you could do. You become stronger than you thought you ever could be.

"There are no shortcuts. It's hard. I love it."

CrossFit isn't easy. While not everybody is as strong as soldier Joseph Schlank, pushing yourself is important. CrossFit instructors are there to help with form and support.

Love didn't come at first sight. Lee arrived at the Okinawa gym that first day not sure what to expect. She did a demo to evaluate her fitness.

"I thought, 'Oh my God.' It was hard."

Still, she kept coming back. She would train for three straight days, rest a day, then train for three more. She improved, but she didn't become a CrossFit wonder overnight.

"When I started, I was sedentary. I had no muscles. I was completely weak. I set a goal of doing five strict push-ups. After five weeks I was seeing the fruits of my labor."

About ten years earlier Lee had hurt her shoulder doing indoor rock climbing. "It got so bad," she says, "they were going to do surgery."

CrossFit training took care of that.

"I never had the surgery or any more problems."

Does Lee push herself hard? You bet she does, sometimes to the point of almost being sick. The satisfaction and resulting good feeling—almost like a runner's high—makes it worth it.

"You get to the end and you can say, 'I got a PR [personal record] today,' or, 'Oh, wow, I never thought I could do that.'"

Now, she does what most people wouldn't think of doing during her four-days-a-week training. On the fourth day, she often adds yoga to her workout.

"I don't work out on the weekend. You have to give muscles a chance to recover. It's possible to do too much."

Lee got her teenaged sons Eric and Thomas to try CrossFit, with mixed results.

"Eric loved it. Thomas didn't. He got frustrated and mad with how he was doing his clean. He didn't like Mom telling him he's not doing it right."

There is an art to working with teenagers and younger kids.

"You don't have kids doing box jumps until they throw up," Lee says. "It's not, 'Okay, game on.' It's fun. It's learning how to do a proper squat or a proper push-up. Imagine an eight-year-old doing pull-ups."

Lee has seen kids pushed to the breaking point, and wants no part of that. "I remember seeing a little girl gymnast with knee and ankle problems. It was already wearing out her joints."

She says it's important to modify workouts for kids or teenagers. Instead of five rounds, you do three. Instead of twenty-five-pound kettlebells, use five pounds. "You change the weight and reps to make it best for them," Lee said.

"I want to be physically fit. I want my kids to be fit, but I don't want it to be all about 'win, win, win.' I know that's a very anti-American way of thinking, but it's about doing something for a lifetime. My dad is eighty and he swims every day."

Lee, forty-five years old in the fall of 2014, says she plans on doing CrossFit "for the rest of my life. I've seen pictures of grandmothers doing deadlifts. I can't imagine not doing it."

Nobody lifts weights alone in CrossFit competitions. A little coaching and encouragement can go a long way.

Her training partner, Kara, is also a forty-something mother. "I find it very empowering," Lee says. "I was in my early forties and I thought it was the start of the end. Now, it's more like the beginning. It's amazing what I can do now. This middle age thing is a bunch of hooey!

"When anything pops up in life, I feel confident I can deal with it. There is nothing I can't try."

How to Pick a Box

So you have decided to try out CrossFit, and need to know where to go. You can go to map.crossfit.com to find boxes near you. The easier a gym is to get to, the more likely you'll be consistent about going. But that's just part of the equation.

"Not all boxes are created equal," Lee Stewart says. "Talk to the trainer in charge. When you're throwing around a hundred or two hundred pounds, and you're not being properly supervised, you can do some damage.

"All my boxes and trainers were great."

Make sure coaches are certified and knowledgeable, and that they are focused on form and doing exercises the right way. Watch to see that coaches are paying attention to the people in their class, and correcting form when necessary. Find out how long they've been doing CrossFit, and how long they've been coaching it. Do they have other fitness training certifications?

Check to see what kind of equipment the box offers. Look for things like pull-up bars, squat racks, rowers, rings, kettlebells, jump ropes, plyo boxes, free weights, medicine balls, and even big truck tires. Make sure that the gym is safe and well-maintained.

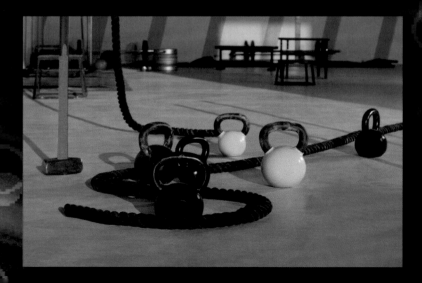

You never know what surprises CrossFit has for you. Some workouts might include shaking heavy ropes, an exercise which works the legs, arms, and core.

Chapter 5
Focus and Passion

Dawn is hours away and Lauren Lowrey faces the television studio spotlight with sparkling dark eyes, enlightening words and, when appropriate, dazzling smiles and sympathetic gestures. She is a popular Indianapolis WISH-TV morning anchor and no one watches to see her blink—or yawn, or stumble, or otherwise mess up.

Lauren's career depends, in part, on looking and feeling her best under harsh television lights, starting at 4:30 in the morning, five days a week. Focus, passion, and energy are critical. Fatigue can't happen.

Lauren trains five to six days a week to make sure that it doesn't, although her motivation goes beyond that. She is attractive, fit, fun, and successful. She is, in many ways, the perfect role model for young girls and, yes, young boys too.

CrossFit has helped.

Today at Lauren's CrossFit box, a leanly muscled instructor with buzzed hair and a sweat-stained gray t-shirt shouts motivational words in a raw voice ("Keep it up!" and "You can do this!"), blowing the whistle that hangs from his neck for emphasis. Ten or so people do as they are told.

Rebelling is not an option.

"It's what you'd think basic training would be like in the Army," Lauren says. "What's crazy is that, with that motivation, you can take a twenty-minute workout and be more zapped than if you had an hour and a half of lower-intensity stuff. It's incredible."

Lauren, who was twenty-nine in the summer of 2014, actually heard about CrossFit through her work. She reported

on a fundraiser for an Indianapolis police officer killed in the line of duty. He had been a "CrossFit fanatic."

Lauren tried it and some of the exercises seemed, well, extreme. There was tire flipping and upside down push-ups (with feet against a wall for support) and box jumps. "Oh, yeah, it can be intimidating at first, but then you see so many other people doing it," Lauren says. "It's like, 'if they can do it, I can do it.'"

"The upside down push-ups seemed bizarre. You don't know if you can do them. They're just awkward. And the tire flipping—I know it seems very simple, but you have to use every muscle in your body."

Workouts vary constantly to challenge your body as well as your mind. According to Greg Glassman, CrossFit prepares participants "not only for the unknown, but for the unknowable as well."

One day, for instance, you might do a WOD called "Jackie." You are timed while you row one thousand meters, then do fifty reps of thrusters with a forty-five-pound bar. That's where you hold a barbell at shoulder level, drop to a squat, then move up to a standing position, pushing the barbell above your head as you go. Then you do thirty pull-ups.

If that sounds tough, well, it is. And when you finally have the strength to handle that, a new challenge comes.

"One of the things that makes CrossFit so appealing," Lauren says, "is that you never master it. There's always room to keep growing. There's a fun, edgy side to it."

Lauren has done some local CrossFit challenges, but "nowhere close to the CrossFit stuff you see on TV." Even regular WODs can turn into competitive battles, though.

"It's like a time trial, you're racing against the other people to see how much you can get done," Lauren says. "When you force your body to do things so quickly, you get more muscle growth."

Lauren danced, sung, and acted professionally (she was a Florida State University theater major) before switching to television news reporting. But growing up in an active and fit environment made CrossFit a natural choice for her. "In my mind, [being active and taking care of yourself] is what you're supposed to do. Not to mention that's what I have to do to keep working."

Tire flipping is a common CrossFit exercise. Competitions push participants to find their limits, as they complete exercises like this one as quickly as possible to beat out other competitors.

Lauren isn't chained to the anchor desk. She often goes outside to do stories. When she was in Myrtle Beach, South Carolina, she spent thirteen hours outside covering hurricanes on two occasions. It required fearlessness and fitness.

It's an approach Lauren has no plans to change.

"I do not subscribe to the theory that when you get older, you're not supposed to move, or you're impaired. I live my

Box jumps are among the ways CrossFit challenges your strength, fitness, and agility.

life under the hypothesis that if I keep moving and vary the ways in which I work out, that won't happen to me."

And so Lauren stays on the move and doesn't look back.

"I want to have kids some day. I want to be able to look the same way when I have kids. Many women say that your body is not the same after having a baby, but I don't agree with that. Plenty of women have bangin' bodies after having kids."

She pauses.

"It only takes a little time, but you can get a great workout."

CrossFit Games

Do you want to be the fittest man or woman on earth? Then take a shot at the CrossFit Games, which draws competitors from all over the world. It's definitely not easy, though, when your competition includes athletes like Rich Froning and Annie Thorisdottir. Froning, who lives in Tennessee, won the men's competition in 2011, 2012, and 2013. Icelander Thorisdottir took the women's titles in 2011 and 2012, but couldn't compete in 2013 because of an injury.

The CrossFit Games began in 2007 and have grown more popular each year. The Games last three days (or more) in July and are held at the StubHub Center in Carson, California. ESPN televises the Games, and Reebok is the Games' official sponsor. Events change each year; competitors don't know exactly what they'll have to do until just before the competition starts.

Events have interesting names such as Naughty Nancy, the Cinco, and Burden Run. Competitors might have to do handstand walks or handstand push-ups, or use weights that weigh hundreds of pounds.

Doing well in the Games can pay off. The winning man and woman each received $275,000 in 2013. Second place was worth $65,000. Third earned the competitor $35,000.

Where to Get Started

So you want to try CrossFit yourself? Be sure to discuss it with your parents and get their permission. Start by looking for gyms/boxes in your area. You can find these online at map.crossfit.com. See "How to Pick a Box" in Chapter 4 for more information. Some gyms have special offers to attract new members. These might be available just by asking at the gym, or through companies like Groupon and LivingSocial. Don't pick a gym based on price alone, though. It is worth paying a little extra for high-quality instruction that will help you avoid injuries.

Before you start, you'll want to get comfortable workout clothes and supportive shoes. You can also research workouts and general information about CrossFit so you know what to look for in a good box. For information on CrossFit, go to www.crossfit.com and www.crossfitkids.com. Check out "Further Reading" in the back of this book to learn more about Crossfit, the Paleo Diet, and general fitness.

1974	Crossfit founder Greg Glassman gets his first training job at eighteen years old—coaching gymnastics at the YWCA in Pasadena, California.
1974–1989	Glassman trains celebrities and athletes at multiple Southern California gyms. He begins achieving success with short, efficient, high-intensity workouts. He works with police officers and creates his own training system that combines elements of bodybuilding and endurance conditioning.
1995	Glassman is hired to train the Santa Cruz, California, police department. He also opens the first CrossFit gym in Santa Cruz. During this time CrossFit starts generating television, radio, and print attention because of the benefits local police officers are seeing.
2001	Glassman launches crossfit.com to provide Internet access to his program. It features a Workout of the Day (WOD), plus offers a library of workout and exercise demo videos. There's an active discussion forum where people can talk about various CrossFit topics.
2003	CrossFit begins its affiliate program, which allows independent gyms to be certified by CrossFit. By 2005, there are eighteen CrossFit-sanctioned gyms.
2005 to present	Affiliate gym growth takes place all over the United States and beyond.
2007	The CrossFit Games are founded to identify the nation's fittest man and woman based on CrossFit standards.
2009	There are over one thousand CrossFit affiliates worldwide.
2012	There are 3,400 CrossFit affiliates worldwide.
2013	Three-time CrossFit Games Champion Rich Froning releases his memoir, *First: What It Takes to Win*.
2014	Cirque du Soleil trainer Allister Booth begins using CrossFit to keep cast members in shape.

PHOTO CREDITS: All design elements from Thinkstock/Sharon Beck; Cover, p. 1—Photos.com/Thinkstock; pp. 4-5, 6, 11, 19, 29, 35, 36, 42—Thinkstock; p. 9—courtesy of Sarah Hoffman; p. 10—David Bro/ZUMA Press/Newscom; p. 12—US Army, 12; p. 14—Staff Sgt. Clinton Firstbrook; pp. 16-17—Spc. James Wilton; p. 18—Mass Communication Specialist 2nd Class Eddie Harrison; p. 20—Craig Cunningham/Charleston Daily Mail/AP Images; pp. 22-23—Debbie Noda/ZUMAPRESS/Newscom; pp. 25, 30—Pete DiPrimio; pp. 26-27—Cpl. Meg Murray; p. 32—Senior Airman Dennis Sloan; p. 34—Maj. Lindy White; p. 39—Spc. Emily Knitter, 1/3 HBCT; p. 40—Cerri, Lara/ZUMA Press/Newscom; p. 41—Greg Lovett/ZUMAPRESS/Newscom

Books

Chapman, Doug. *Training for the CrossFit Games*. Ann Arbor, MI: HyperFit System, Inc., 2013.

Faigenbaum, Avery, and Wayne Westcott. *Youth Strength Training*. Champaign, IL: Human Kinetics, 2009.

Holden, Marc. *W.O.D for Beginners: Get Muscle, Strength, and Stamina in 30 Minutes or Less*. Las Vegas: CreateSpace, 2013.

Wenglin Belger, Allison. *The Power of Community: CrossFit and the Force of Human Connection*. Las Vegas: Victory Belt Publishing, 2012.

Wolf, Robb. *The Paleo Solution*. Las Vegas: Victory Belt Publishing, 2010.

On The Internet

CrossFit: Forging Elite Fitness
    http://www.crossfit.com/

CrossFit Kids: Forging the Future of Fitness
    http://www.crossfitkids.com/

FitDay: Free Calorie Counter & Weight-Loss Journal
    http://www.fitday.com/

Works Consulted

Charge CrossFit. http://www.chargecrossfit.com.au/

Craw, Victoria. "Meet Greg Glassman, the Man behind the CrossFit Machine." News.com.au, October 25, 2013. http://www.news.com.au/business/companies/meet-greg-glassman-the-man-behind-the-crossfit-machine/story-fnda1bsz-1226746475853

CrossFit. "CrossFit Sweetens the Pot for the 2013 Reebok CrossFit Games." Reebok CrossFit Games, July 3, 2013. http://games.crossfit.com/article/crossfit-sweetens-pot-2013-reebok-crossfit-games

CrossFit, "CrossFit Training Courses." http://www.crossfit.com/cf-info/certs.shtml

CrossFit. "History: Finding the Fittest on Earth." Reebok CrossFit Games. http://games.crossfit.com/about-the-games/history

CrossFit Iota. "Brief History of CrossFit." http://crossfitiota.com/about-us/brief-history-of-crossfit/

CrossFit. "Regional Events." Reebok CrossFit Games. http://games.crossfit.com/workouts/regionals

CrossFit Virtuosity. "Greg Glassman Biography." http://www.crossfitvirtuosity.com/assets/glassman_factsheet.pdf

Etchecolatz, Facundo, and Megan Mitchell. "CrossFit Goes Global." Reebok CrossFit Games, November 8, 2011. http://games.crossfit.com/article/crossfit-goes-global

Gay, Jason. "Sean Payton's Heavy Lift: CrossFit." *Wall Street Journal,* October 11, 2013. http://online.wsj.com/news/articles/SB10001424052702304500404579129521880382800

Glassman, Greg. "Understanding CrossFit." *CrossFit Journal,* April 1, 2007. http://journal.crossfit.com/2007/04/understanding-crossfit-by-greg.tpl

Goldsborough, Jaclyn. "Downtown Fort Wayne's New CrossFit Gym to Hold Grand Opening." *Fort Wayne News-Sentinel,* September 10, 2013.

Greenfest, Sara. "9 Strong Stars Who Love CrossFit Workouts." *Men's Fitness*. http://www.mensfitness.com/training/9-strong-stars-who-love-crossfit

Hallowell, Billy. "CrossFit Founder Unabashedly Discusses His Politics: 'I'm a Rabid Libertarian.'" The Blaze, July 23, 2013. http://www.theblaze.com/stories/2013/07/23/crossfit-founder-unabashedly-discusses-his-politics-im-a-rabid-libertarian/

Hoffman, Sarah (Denison University track and field athlete and CrossFit participant). Interview with the author, October 2013.

Huffington Post. "Crossfit: Miss America Mallory Hagan and Other Celebrities Who Love the Workout." January 15, 2013. http://www.huffingtonpost.com/2013/01/15/crossfit-miss-america-mallory-hagan_n_2473252.html

Innis Tieman, Jenna (CrossFit certified instructor and co-owner of Hoosier CrossFit in Bloomington, IN). Interview with the author, November 2013.

Lowrey, Lauren (Indianapolis TV morning anchor and CrossFit participant). Interview with the author, July 2013.

New York Post. "B'klyn's Own Miss America: I Understand Hardships Women Face." January 14, 2013. http://nypost.com/2013/01/14/bklyns-own-miss-america-i-understand-hardships-women-face/

The Paleo Diet. "What to Eat on the Paleo Diet." http://thepaleodiet.com/what-to-eat-on-the-paleo-diet/

Robertson, Eric. "CrossFit's Dirty Little Secret." *HuffPost Healthy Living,* September 24, 2013. http://www.huffingtonpost.com/eric-robertson/crossfit-rhabdomyolysis_b_3977598.html?utm_hp_ref=mostpopular

Stewart, Lee (CrossFit certified instructor). Interview with the author, September 2013.

Warkentin, Mike. "Mads Scientist." Reebok CrossFit Games, October 30, 2013. http://games.crossfit.com/article/mads-scientist

Glossary of Exercises

air squat—Athlete moves from the standing position with toes pointed slightly outward to a squatting position with the hips below the knees, then back to standing. While squatting, knees should be turned slightly out, above the toes. Weight should rest on the heels.

box jump—From a standing position on the floor, the athlete jumps and lands with both feet on top of a box, and stands straight up before returning to the floor. Typical box heights in inches are 15", 20", 24", and 30".

burpee—Beginning in a standing position, the athlete drops to the floor with the feet extending backward, touches the floor with the chest, and then pulls the legs forward, landing in a squatting position before jumping up and then standing.

clean—Start with a deadlift, then at the top of the deadlift, jump and bring the barbell into a rack position (on the shoulders in front of the neck). Land your jump by squatting down with the barbell in the front squat position, then drive up to standing position.

deadlift—Standing with feet just under the barbell, lift the barbell from the ground. Make sure to drive with the legs and glutes, until reaching an upright standing position.

front squat—Similar to an air squat, but a barbell is held in the "rack position" (on the shoulders, in front of the neck), with the hands on the bar and forearms facing the ceiling.

handstand push-up—Beginning in a handstand, with the arms straight and (usually) the heels gently resting against a wall, the athlete bends the arms until the head touches the ground, and then pushes back up into a handstand position.

kettlebell swing—A kettlebell is swung from between the legs to eye level (Russian) or overhead (American).

medicine ball clean—With feet wide, bend knees and lift medicine ball from the floor. Stand straight, then squat down, bringing medicine ball in front of the upper chest. Stand up.

overhead squat—Same as air squat, but with barbell held overhead. Elbows are straight throughout the squat.

press—Barbell is moved from the "rack position" (on shoulders, in front of the neck) to the overhead position. In a shoulder press, the lower body remains stationary. In a push press, the bar is pushed off the body using the hips and legs. Knees are slightly bent, then straightened as the bar is pushed up. A push jerk is like a push press, but with a jump. A push jerk is landed with knees slightly bent before standing straight.

pull-up—The athlete begins hanging from a bar with hands gripping the bar and palms facing forward. The athlete pulls up until the chin is over the bar, then returns to starting position.

push-up—Starting in a plank position with the arms straight, the athlete lowers until the chest makes contact with the ground, keeping the body straight throughout, and making sure the elbows track straight back instead of out, then pushes back up into the plank position.

rope climb—Starting from the ground, the athlete climbs a rope and touches a point at a specific height.

rowing—A workout using a rowing machine, which duplicates the motion of rowing a boat. Works the arms, chest, shoulders, legs, and hips.

sumo deadlift high pull—With a wide stance, a barbell or kettlebell is lifted from the ground to a position just under the chin. Elbows stay above the hands.

thruster—A combination of a front squat and a push press: starting with the barbell in the rack position, the athlete squats and then stands, driving the barbell overhead.

tire flip—A large tire, lying on its side, is flipped over by lifting one edge.

wall ball—Holding a medicine ball below the chin while facing a wall at arm's length, the athlete squats and stands, throwing the medicine ball in order to make contact with an overhead target on the wall.

Glossary

agility (uh-JIL-i-tee)—The ability to move quickly and easily.

box—A licensed CrossFit affiliate gym.

cardiovascular (kahr-dee-oh-VAS-kyuh-ler)—Related to the heart and blood vessels; a cardiovascular exercise works the heart and blood vessels.

coordination (koh-awr-din-EY-shuhn)—The use of different body parts together for a single purpose.

core—The muscles of the torso, including the abdominals and back muscles.

endurance (en-DOOR-uhns)—The ability to keep going under difficult conditions.

scholarship (SKOL-er-ship)—Money given to a student to attend a school based on talent, achievements, or financial need.

stamina (STAM-uh-nuh)—Strength or ability to keep going when sick or tired.

triathlon (trahy-ATH-luhn)—A competition consisting of three events, usually swimming, bicycling, and running.

Index

About the Author

Pete DiPrimio is an award-winning Indiana sports writer, a long-time freelance writer, and a veteran children's author. He's also a journalism adjunct lecturer and a fitness instructor.